SAVE THE CHILDREN

LOUISE SPILSBURY

Heinemann
LIBRARY

www.heinemann.co.uk

Visit our website to find out more information about **Heinemann Library** books.

To order:

 Phone +44 (0) 1865 888066

 Send a fax to +44 (0) 1865 314091

 Visit the Heinemann Bookshop at www.heinemann.co.uk to browse our catalogue and order online.

First published in Great Britain by Heinemann Library, Halley Court, Jordan Hill, Oxford OX2 8EJ, a division of Reed Educational and Professional Publishing Ltd. Heinemann is a registered trademark of Reed Educational & Professional Publishing Ltd.

OXFORD MELBOURNE AUCKLAND JOHANNESBURG BLANTYRE
GABORONE IBADAN PORTSMOUTH NH (USA) CHICAGO

Designed by Ken Vail Graphic Design, Cambridge
Originated by Universal Colour Scanning
Printed by Wing King Tong in Hong Kong

ISBN 0 431 02737 4
04 03 02 01 00
10 9 8 7 6 5 4 3 2 1

Heinemann Library paid a contribution to Save the Children for their help in the creation of this book.

British Library Cataloguing in Publication Data
Spilsbury, Louise
Save the Children – (Taking Action!)
1.Save the Children – Juvenile literature
I.Title
361.7'63'0941

Acknowledgements
The Publishers would like to thank the following for permission to reproduce photographs:
Antonia Reeve Photography pp12 all, 13; Howard Davies/STC p5 upper; Peter Fryer/STC pp 9 right, 29 upper; Mike Goldwater/STC/Network p24; Alec Lessin/STC pp14 all, 15 upper, 30; Jenny Matthews/STC pp 8 upper, 9 left, 24 lower, 27 upper, 29 main; Jenny Matthews/STC/Network pp 4 lower, 20, 21; Dario Mitidieri/STC pp9 main, 18, 28 upper; Caroline Penn/STC p19; Jon Spaull/STC p10 lower; Liba Taylor/STC pp5 lower, 22, 23, 25 lower; Penny Tweedie/STC pp7 lower, 28 lower, 29 lower; Simon Wood/STC p26.
All other photographs reproduced by permission of Save the Children.

Cover illustration by Scott Rhodes.

Cover photograph reproduced with permission of Save the Children (Howard Davies).

Our thanks to staff at Save the Children for their help in the preparation of this book.

Every effort has been made to contact copyright holders of any material reproduced in this book. Any omissions will be rectified in subsequent printings if notice is given to the Publisher.

Photographs are not necessarily of the children whose stories appear in this book. Details of some children's stories have been changed to protect their identities.

Words appearing in the text in bold, **like this**, are explained in the Glossary.

CONTENTS

WHAT'S THE PROBLEM?

Many children in the UK and across the world are not getting the start in life that they deserve. Some children – the lucky ones – lead mostly safe, happy and healthy lives with plenty of chances to learn and develop, and the freedom to make choices about who they are and what they want to be. But for many children this is simply not the case.

Every day thousands of children are not given the food they need to grow up healthy and strong. Many die or are left frail and weak by hunger or by diseases that could have been cured. Some don't get the chance to go to school, perhaps because they work long hours to help feed and clothe their families, or there are no good schools nearby. Some of those who go to school may find it impossible to learn because of bullying or **abuse**. Children's lives are disrupted in many ways by wars and **natural disasters**, in which they may be separated from their families, injured or even killed.

Poverty is the biggest danger facing the world's children today. In Ethiopia, some families from the countryside are so poor that they are forced to leave their children in towns. They know that their children have more chance of scraping a living through begging in the city streets.

In many countries children only go to school a little, if at all. This may be because school fees are too expensive or the schools too far away. Or it may be that children have to work during school hours.

4

There are about 2.3 billion children in the world.

Once it was only soldiers who died in war. Today, most victims are ordinary people, and many of these are children. This boy fled to a *refugee* camp, where he was given food and shelter.

◄ We take drinking and bath water for granted. Turn on a tap, and there it is. For many children around the world it is difficult to find water that is safe to drink. Many children spend much of their time collecting water from pools or drains for their families.

Children make up 40% of the world's population.

SAVE THE CHILDREN

THEN AND NOW

Save the Children began its work in 1919, just after World War I. Britain and its **allies** were stopping food getting through to Austria, Hungary and Germany – the countries they had defeated. They wanted to force these countries to sign a **peace treaty**. But thousands of children there were starving. Eglantyne Jebb, who had already done some **charity** work helping **refugees**, wanted to do something to help. She and her sister Dorothy Buxton started a fund to raise money. At first, some people were angry that they wanted to help Britain's former enemies. Jebb had to put up with a lot of criticism, but she also persuaded thousands of people to send money to help 'save the children'.

THE RIGHTS OF THE CHILD

It was one thing raising support for an emergency, but what about the suffering and **poverty** that the world's children faced every day? In response to these problems, Eglantyne Jebb wrote a declaration in 1923 – a set of simple statements demanding certain **children's rights**. This was adopted by the **League of Nations** in 1924 and

Eglantyne Jebb was a remarkable woman with a powerful personality. She firmly believed that children should be helped not only in times of crisis, but by giving them and their families the means to help themselves every day.

eventually became part of international law as the **United Nations Convention on the Rights of the Child** in 1989.

Since 1919 Save the Children has worked in over 130 countries around the world.

SAVE THE CHILDREN TODAY

All of Save the Children's work today is based on the United Nations Convention on the Rights of the Child. As well as being the UK's largest international charity working with children, it is part of the International Save the Children Alliance – a partnership of Save the Children organizations around the world. At a time when many children are still denied the basic rights which Eglantyne Jebb fought for, Save the Children is working to create a world where all children have the chance of a safe, happy and secure childhood.

In 1920 Eglantyne Jebb published advertisements in national newspapers 'to touch the imagination of the world'. No charity had ever done this before and people thought she was wasting money. But it worked – *donations* began pouring in from supporters.

Eglantyne Jebb once wrote: 'The only international language is a child's cry'. Save the Children believes that all children have the right to help whenever they need it.

Today, Save the Children works in about 70 countries around the world, including the UK.

WHAT DOES SAVE THE CHILDREN DO?

Children are at the heart of everything Save the Children does. The starting point for any of the **charity's** work is children themselves – what they say their situation is, what they say they need and what they think should be done to solve their problems. Save the Children then uses this knowledge to develop realistic, long-term solutions which help children and their families help themselves. Save the Children does not just give people things; it works to create a world in which children and their families are able to take control of their own lives.

These children at a *refugee* camp in Macedonia are playing with toys supplied by Save the Children. By playing, children can regain a feeling of normality and forget the misery of their situation for a while.

CAMPAIGNS

Save the Children supports projects in the UK and across the world. It uses the experience and expertise gained from this work in its **campaigns**. Campaigns are a way of speaking out for children, to inform all sorts of people – parents, teachers, communities, governments – about children's needs and rights. Campaigns are also essential for making people understand that their help is needed and to show them ways in which they can help – from ordinary people giving **donations** of money or **volunteering** their time, to government action on improving laws which protect **children's rights**.

Save the Children employs around 4000 staff in the UK and overseas.

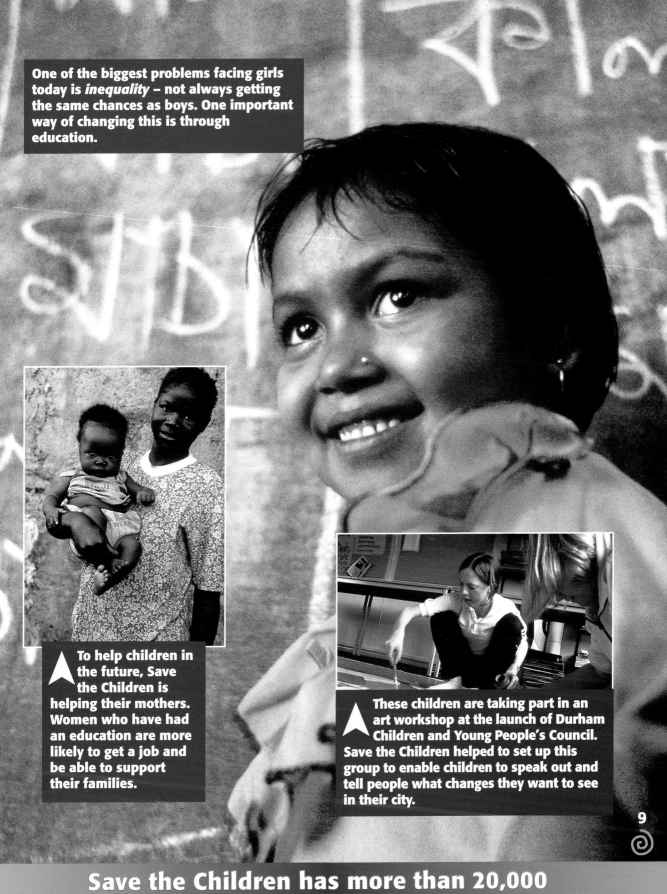

One of the biggest problems facing girls today is *inequality* – not always getting the same chances as boys. One important way of changing this is through education.

▲ To help children in the future, Save the Children is helping their mothers. Women who have had an education are more likely to get a job and be able to support their families.

▲ These children are taking part in an art workshop at the launch of Durham Children and Young People's Council. Save the Children helped to set up this group to enable children to speak out and tell people what changes they want to see in their city.

9

Save the Children has more than 20,000 volunteers in the UK.

MEET OYUNBILEG RENTSENDORJIIN

PROJECT WORKER

9am I have a meeting about a training programme for 17 local government officers in a province in eastern Mongolia. These officers will be responsible for supporting children and their families. We're helping the officers find out who the families should contact for the particular help they need.

▼ **I spend a lot of time talking to children and their families at home, at work, or in their villages to find out how they think Save the Children can help them.**

Many children in Mongolia lack the things we take for granted, like food, clothing and shelter. I work for Save the Children in Mongolia to help children and their families. One of the projects I work on is to help mothers find ways of earning money to support themselves and their children. Another is to train older children with skills that will help them organize their personal lives later. I also work in a team that is helping to ease the problem of **poverty** in Mongolia. We work with the government on ways of helping poor families.

Save the Children helps parents to buy shoes for their children so that they can attend school.

11am Back at the office, I arrange for the British Ambassador to meet some children. The UK government gives Save the Children money for its work in Mongolia. The Ambassador works for the UK government, and comes to see how the money is being spent.

12 noon I visit a secondary school to discuss training sessions there. By supporting teachers, and giving them information about **children's rights**, we suggest new ways of working with children. They can then help the children become more confident about expressing their views.

2pm After lunch, I go to a meeting with someone from the central government office that decides how best to help children in very poor families. We plan to meet people in communities and find out how to help.

4pm I check on a service centre for street children. There are six helpers at the centre. They provide children who live on the street with helpful information — like how to prevent diseases.

▶ **This picture by a child in Mongolia shows what it's like to live and beg on the streets in a country where temperatures can drop as low as -20°C, which is way below freezing.**

In Mongolia, Save the Children supports shelters for over 200 street children.

MEET SHAMYLLA SYED

COMMUNITY WORKER

My name is Shamylla Syed, and I'm 18 years old. I'm working on a project about **racism** and bullying in schools, youth clubs and communities. I'm based at a youth club for under-18s in Edinburgh. Save the Children helped to fund my project and the training I needed to get started.

My research in local schools showed me that almost all children experience bullying or racism at some time in their lives. I've been a victim of both in the past, and I want to help children speak out about their fears. When it happened to me I had no one to tell. I don't want the same happening to any other child.

9am It's Friday today and time for a meeting with the other staff who run the youth club. We talk about our plans for next week and discuss any problems we may have had. I ask if anyone will be able to help run my drama club next week.

1pm I use my half-hour lunch break to check my e-mails. A lot of these are from people around Edinburgh and across the UK who are working on similar projects. This keeps me up-to-date with what's happening in the rest of the country.

1.30pm Now it's time for my drama club. I organize this club because it's a great chance for young people from the local community to share their experiences and ideas. We're working together to create a show about racism and bullying in children's lives.

► As part of Eid, a *Muslim* festival week, I did hand-painting with the drama group. This also gave us a quiet time to talk.

Shamylla's research showed that one in two secondary schoolchildren had been bullied.

3pm We take a break from rehearsals and discuss the aims of the show. We talk about the kinds of racism and bullying we have experienced ourselves and about what we can all do to stop these forms of **abuse**.

4pm When everyone else has left, I stay behind to write notes about the session. I keep careful records of what we do because it's good to look back and see how the young people I've been working with have changed over the year, and to see if I've helped them to work out ways of dealing with racism and bullying.

In the drama rehearsals and performances young people have the chance to act out things that have happened to them.

Almost a third of the bullied children said that they were less able to concentrate on their work.

MEET LEIGH DAYNES

PRESS OFFICER

As press officer, it's my job to get news about Save the Children into the **media**. It's really important that as many people as possible understand that many children don't enjoy their right to a happy, healthy and safe childhood.

I really like my job because I get to do lots of very different things. I help children and young people have a say in the news; I provide journalists with ideas for newspaper, radio or television features; and I visit Save the Children projects, so that I can tell other people about the way children are improving life in their own communities.

8.30am I start the day by reading the newspapers to see what's happening in the world that might affect children.

9.30am I write and send out letters to journalists about a group of young people who are going to talk to government **ministers** about what it's like to be a **refugee**. I hope this will encourage them to tell this important story in their newspapers.

11am At a staff meeting we discuss our plans for the coming weeks. I'm planning to invite a journalist and a photographer to go to Ethiopia to see the problems children face in getting proper healthcare.

This is me in my office. I'm talking to a co-worker and a student who is with us for some work experience.

In developing countries, 110 million children of primary school age don't go to school.

12.30pm I visit BBC Television Centre in west London, where I talk to my friends at 'Newsround'. They are going to include a piece in their teatime show about what Save the Children is doing in the UK.

▶ **As part of my job, I do interviews for television and radio about children's issues. Here I'm chatting with the presenter of _Newsround_, the news programme on Children's BBC. We're talking about the item he'll be featuring on Save the Children.**

▲ **The football coach and sports commentator John Barnes came to the launch of 'Read me another, Dad!' This is our campaign to encourage dads to read to their sons more often. Our research suggests that this might encourage boys to read more themselves.**

2.30pm Back in the office, I talk to our Director General about a press conference I have arranged for him tomorrow. He is going to tell journalists about our **campaign** to make people aware of the suffering of children caught up in the wars and conflicts going on around the world today.

3.30pm At a team meeting, we talk about all the excellent publicity we have had in the media about our new book encouraging dads to read with their sons.

6pm I go back to the BBC to watch some films made by children from different parts of Europe. The films are a result of a project partly funded by Save the Children. Young people were encouraged to make videos about issues that concerned them, like **racism** and bullying. The films are excellent — but I'm quite tired by the time I get home!

15

275 million children in developing countries don't go to secondary school.

MEET NICHOLA JAMES
FUND-RAISING MANAGER

As fund-raising manager it's my job to come up with exciting ideas to encourage people in Northern Ireland to give money to Save the Children. It's incredibly satisfying to know that the work I do with the **volunteers** here in Belfast helps children across the world. It's also great fun! I've dressed up as a Japanese dancing girl to draw attention to an event; I've been **sponsored** to climb the highest mountains in Wales and Ireland to raise funds; and I've even persuaded my husband to visit a Save the Children project while we were on honeymoon in Tanzania!

9.30am Today is the beginning of Save the Children Week — probably the busiest fund-raising week of the year. Every volunteer group and shop across Northern Ireland is doing something to help. This morning I'm helping to sort out street and house-to-house collections and special events. We're also arranging to send a letter to every house in Northern Ireland asking for people's support.

10.30am I spend a couple of hours dealing with my e-mails. These are invaluable — they give me up-to-the-minute information about the things Save the Children is doing all over the world. This means I can

These children have kindly put some money in a volunteer's collection tin. Save the Children Week is a great chance to raise money and make people aware of the important work we do.

Save the Children runs more than 150 shops in the UK, staffed by volunteers.

tell our volunteers exactly how the money they are raising is being spent. A supporter writes asking how much this Week will raise. I tell her that it usually raises around £60,000 in Northern Ireland and just under £1 million across the UK.

12.30pm The theme for this year's Week is children forced out of their homes because of war — there are an incredible 20 million of them around the world. As well as the fund-raising this week, I'm helping to organize a **campaign** on this theme. We hope to make more people aware of this problem and get them to take action to help. Instead of getting people to sign their names in support of the campaign, we're asking them to give or send us photos of themselves instead!

This is me climbing Snowdon with some other volunteers. As well as raising money for Save the Children, we had a great day out and the sun even shone for us!

2pm I take to the streets with other members of staff to help out with the street collection in Belfast city centre. It can be hard work but most people are very generous and you can make up to £30 an hour.

4pm I leave the others to visit a local school to give a talk about Save the Children to a small group of sixth-form A level Home Economics students. I bring a student with me who is spending some time at the Save the Children offices for work experience. She's surprised that I'm happy to spend so much time talking about Save the Children and the charity's work in general, and not just about fund-raising.

5.30pm I sort through photos just in of a recent 'Hike to Help' event. Along with some other Save the Children supporters, I climbed Snowdon, the highest mountain in Wales to raise money. It was a great day and since then several of the people who came on the walks have volunteered to help with their local street collection. I spend some time choosing the funniest pictures of all the people who took part and send them out to them as a way of saying thank you for taking part.

17

There are around 650 Save the Children volunteer groups around the UK.

WORK WITH YOUNG DECISION-MAKERS

If there is a decision to be made about your life or your future, don't you think you have the right to take part in that decision? After all, no one knows as well as you how you feel about something. Before taking action, Save the Children always listens to what children say and what they think should be done about an issue or a situation. Solutions to problems are worked out with children and young people, not for them.

STREETWISE

Reema is only 11, but she's seen more of life than many adults. At seven, she left her home in Bangladesh's countryside to work in the capital city, Dhaka. She got work as a maid, but her employers mistreated her. So she ran away and slept on the streets. When the police found her, they put her in prison. Reema is now out of jail and she's joined a group of street children brought together by Save the Children. She and the other street children have written a report about the unfair way they are treated by the police. They've spoken at meetings to

These Bangladeshi street children are at school in a special centre partly paid for by Save the Children. One of the things they learn is that they have a right to take part in decisions affecting their lives. Hopefully, getting an education will give them the confidence to speak out.

get adults to change the law. She hopes for a better life soon. 'I hope I don't have to spend my whole life on the street. I want to study and I want to stand on my own feet.'

The UN Convention on the Rights of the Child has been signed by almost every country in the world.

SPEAKING OUT

On 24 November 1999 a group of 16 young people from England and Wales, aged between 13 and 17, made history. They became the first young people to hold a meeting at the Foreign and Commonwealth Office in London. At a special session, they questioned members of the government on how it has lived up to its responsibilities under the **United Nations Convention on the Rights of the Child**.

The group spent a month investigating four key issues which they felt were especially important: child soldiers, child labour, child participation, and the environment. They interviewed children, businesses, other **charities** and decision-making groups around the world. Using this information, they led a discussion with a **minister**, business leaders and the head of Save the Children. After the meeting, the committee of young people listed their suggestions for change in a report, which they handed to the government. The event proved yet again that young people have a unique contribution to make to discussions on things that affect their lives.

The special session of the Children's Select Committee was held in November 1999 to mark the tenth anniversary of the UN Convention on the Rights of the Child.

19

Children have the right by law to participate fully in decisions on issues that affect them.

WORK ON CHILD LABOUR

Work is a fact of life for millions of children around the world. Some of the work children do may include helping their families around the house, farm or shop, or part-time jobs which they can fit around schoolwork. But sometimes children have to take on longer or harder kinds of work. Even though they may earn very little, their wages may make the difference between starvation and survival for them and their families.

Save the Children believes that children should be protected from dangerous work or work which takes advantage of them, because it pays them too little or works them too hard. But stopping child labour is not always the answer. Sometimes when children lose their jobs, they go hungry or take on worse paid or more harmful work.

Many children work to help their families earn enough money to survive – like this boy selling nuts at a train station in Tajikistan. Save the Children supports projects that enable parents to earn enough money to support their families.

About 120 million children worldwide work full-time and miss out on education.

TACKLING THE CAUSES

Save the Children works in more than 20 countries worldwide to tackle the problem of child labour. The first step is always to talk to children themselves, and to find out why they work and what changes they would like to see happen. Most children say that they have to work to live or to pay for schooling. They ask Save the Children to help them improve things like bad working conditions, long hours, poor wages or ill-treatment.

Save the Children supports organizations across the world which **campaign** for better pay and conditions for both adults and children. It also helps parents to set up their own businesses or farms, so that families can earn enough money to live, without their children going out to work. Loan and savings schemes enable families to put money aside for the future or in case of hard times.

Many children miss school because they have to help out on the farm or in family businesses. Save the Children funds alternative education projects so that children like these can catch up with their schooling at other times of the day.

Worldwide, about 80% of children's work is unpaid.

WORK WITH HIV/AIDS

AIDS is a medical condition caused by a **virus** called HIV. The HIV virus weakens a person's **immune system**, which is supposed to protect the body. This means people with HIV/AIDS get illnesses, such as pneumonia, more easily and have trouble recovering. HIV and AIDS affect children all over the world. Millions are sick or have died as a result of the virus. Others see their loved ones fall ill and die.

PREVENTION

The HIV virus is passed from one person to another through some bodily fluids, including blood, semen and mother's milk. It can be passed on through sexual intercourse or by injecting drugs with a needle that an infected person has used. You cannot get HIV/AIDS by breathing the same air as someone with the virus or by touching them.

It's important that children know about how HIV can be passed on so they can protect themselves against infection. To do this, Save the Children listens to children's and young people's views and experiences of HIV/AIDS. This helps the **charity** provide services which young people feel comfortable using – for instance, by writing leaflets that don't use complicated medical terms. Save the Children runs HIV/AIDS education sessions in schools, youth clubs and health centres. They particularly try to get in touch with children and young people who are most at risk of contracting the disease, such as those living on the streets.

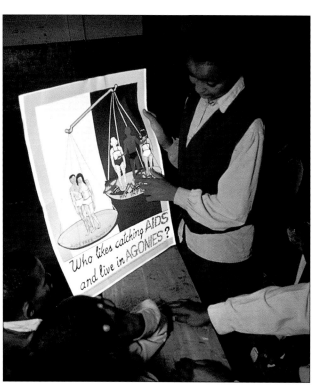

◀ **Children at a junior school in Ethiopia discuss an HIV/AIDS awareness poster. They made it after talking to Save the Children workers about the medical condition.**

One of the biggest problems facing children in the 21st century will be HIV/AIDS.

CARE

Save the Children helps support and care for children and families affected by HIV/AIDS. It works to improve health services and to train people to care for those affected by the disease. Save the Children tries hard to make sure children affected by HIV/AIDS don't get sent away from their homes and communities. For instance, if a child loses his or her parents, the charity works to help that child stay in their own town or village, where things are safe and familiar, instead of being sent away to an orphanage.

Save the Children works with communities to teach them about HIV/AIDS and to encourage people to have a caring and compassionate attitude to those living with the virus.

Save the Children also works with governments in many countries to try to solve problems that make it hard to stop the spread of HIV/AIDS, such as **poverty**. The charity also argues for new treatments to be made available to everyone, rich and poor alike, wherever they live.

Nearly 13 million children have lost their mothers and fathers because of HIV/AIDS.

CHILDREN IN CONFLICTS

Imagine you are a child growing up in a country at war. You never feel safe and you often feel scared. You cannot get to school because the building has been destroyed, and your teacher is missing. Sometimes there is not enough food to eat because the road is blocked and supplies cannot get through to your village. When you are ill, it is difficult to get to a hospital, and medical supplies are running out.

Save the Children helps children who have been soldiers find their families and settle back into normal life. The *charity* runs special centres to give them a chance to learn and play, so that their lives regain some normality.

As well as suffering the daily problems of living in a war zone, some children may see people they love imprisoned, injured or killed. Some children may even become directly involved in the fighting themselves.

CHILD SOLDIERS

Today, armies use children as soldiers in over 30 countries across the world. Children can move quickly, take orders easily, eat less food and can carry lightweight modern weapons. Some children are kidnapped and forced to join armed groups. But many others join up because they are given food, shelter and clothing.

In 1998–1999 1.5 million children were killed in wars.

Save the Children does all it can to help children caught up in conflicts. It works for the release of boys and girls who are being used as soldiers. Then it helps them to recover and catch up with their schoolwork. It also gives them the chance to regain their childhood by being given time to play again. Some children may have lost contact with their families. Save the Children helps them to find their families, and works with them and their communities to settle the children back into their homes.

► **When everything around them is bleak, being able to help rebuild their homes and villages helps children caught up in wars to look forward to the future.**

◄ **This poem was written by Charlotte Brady, a nine-year-old girl from Northern Ireland. If your life sometimes feels boring think of Charlotte's longing for 'the ordinary excitement of an ordinary day'.**

PEACE IN OUR TOWN

No more bombs and bullets
or jumping from my bed
No more midnight explosions
sounding in my head
No more rattlesnake gunfire
with a warning code
No more landrovers
screaming down the road
No more helicopters
in a hospital race
No more frightened people
afraid to show their face

Just the dull ordinary excitement of
an ordinary day.

Charlotte Brady

Worldwide, about 300,000 children – some as young as seven – fight in armed conflicts every day.

FIND OUT MORE

There are lots of ways you can find out more about Save the Children and what the **charity** does. Without the support of people like you, Save the Children could not reach out to all the children who need help.

Information For more details about where Save the Children works and what it does, phone the Public Enquiry Unit on 020 7716 2268.

Read all about it! Save the Children publishes lots of booklets, leaflets and magazines about its work with children around the world – some of them suitable for children. To receive details of these publications, phone 020 7716 2268.

Web wonder Save the Children's website has masses of useful information, including local and national events, the latest news on emergencies around the world, and the opportunity to contact and learn about the lives of children in other countries. Find it on:

www.savethechildren.org.uk

Lessons learnt Save the Children works with children in schools and youth clubs in the UK to promote understanding of children's lives around the world, and make links between children in the UK and elsewhere.

To find out how your school can get in touch, write to the Education Unit, Save the Children, 17 Grove Lane, London SE5 8RD.

Regional fund-raising There are more than 650 local branches of Save the Children **volunteers** which raise funds and **campaign** on behalf of children around the world. Save the Children also runs more than 150 shops throughout the UK.

To find out how you can get involved, phone the volunteer help desk on 020 7716 2217.

▶ Joining in the fun at London's biggest and best-loved charity fund-raising walk, Save the Children's Strollerthon, in July 1999. Starting and finishing near London Zoo in Regent's Park, the Strollerthon takes in 16 kilometres of London's beautiful parks and landmarks.

GLOSSARY

abuse emotional or physical cruelty

allies countries which, with Britain, fought against Germany in World War I

campaigns activities that aim to tell people something, or to get something changed

charity non-profit-making organization set up to help people

children's rights special human rights for children. These include the right to life, good health, a name and identity, and protection from abuse and neglect. Children also have the right to have their views taken into account.

donations gifts of money or goods

immune system body functions which work to prevent us getting ill, such as white blood cells which destroy germs which enter the body

inequality when people are not treated In the same way as others

landmines buried bombs which explode when a person or animal steps on or touches them

League of Nations international peace-keeping body set up after World War I. This was later replaced by the United Nations (UN).

media newspapers, magazines, radio, television, the internet and other ways of communicating with lots of people

ministers people in the government who make decisions about particular issues

Muslim a follower of the religion of Islam

natural disasters disasters caused by nature, such as floods, earthquakes, volcanoes or hurricanes

peace treaty formal agreement of peace between two sides who have been at war

poverty not having enough money to buy the basic necessities of life, such as food, heating and clothes

racism when people are treated badly or unfairly because of their colour, religious beliefs, culture or ethnic origin

refugees people who have had to leave their country and are unable to go back because it is not safe

sponsored when people promise money to a charity for an activity someone else carries out

United Nations (UN) international organization whose purpose is to maintain peace and security around the world

United Nations Convention on the Rights of the Child rules set up in 1989 by the UN about the way children should be treated across the world

virus organism that causes diseases in people, animals and plants

volunteer/volunteering work without being paid

INDEX